n. Washington M. Wa
e ton M. Washington ton
n. Washington ton M. Wa
e ton M. Washington ton
n. Washington ton M. Wa
e ton M. Washington ton
n. Washington ton M. Wa
e ton M. Washington ton
n. Washington ton M. Wa
e ton M. Washington ton
n. Washington ton M. Wa
e ton M. Washington ton
n. Washington ton M. Wa

A SHORT BIOGRAPHY OF MARTHA WASHINGTON

A SHORT BIOGRAPHY OF
Martha Washington

Mary V. Thompson

BENNA BOOKS

Carlisle, Massachusetts

A Short Biography of Martha Washington

Series Editor: Susan DeLand
Written by: Mary V. Thompson

Copyright © 2017 Applewood Books, Inc.

978-1-944038-24-3

Front cover: *Martha Washington,* 1878
Eliphalet Frazer Andrews
Oil on canvas
33.02 cm x 53.31 cm
White House Collection / White House Historical Association
Back cover: *The Republican Court: Lady Washington's Reception* (Detail)
Engraved by Alexander Hay Ritchie, after Daniel Huntington, 1867
Courtesy of Mount Vernon

Published by Benna Books
an imprint of Applewood Books, Inc.
Carlisle, Massachusetts

To request a free copy of our current catalog
featuring our best-selling books, write to:
Applewood Books
P.O. Box 27
Carlisle, Massachusetts 01741
Or visit us on the web at: www.awb.com

10 9 8 7 6 5 4 3 2 1
MANUFACTURED IN THE UNITED STATES OF AMERICA

MARTHA DANDRIDGE, THE VERY first First Lady of the United States, was born on June 2, 1731, at Chestnut Grove, her family's five-hundred-acre plantation on the Pamunkey River in New Kent County, in the British colony of Virginia. Her immigrant father, Colonel John Dandridge, was the son of a craftsman (a painter and stainer) in England and rose to be clerk of the county and a militia officer. Her mother, Frances Jones, was the daughter of a member of the Virginia legislature, known as the House of

Burgesses. Martha's maternal family had long-standing roots in the colonies. Her mother's grandfather, Rowland Jones, being an Anglican minister—the first pastor at Bruton Parish Church in Williamsburg, Virginia—and her great-great-grandfather, William Woodward, a trader with, and interpreter for, Native Americans in the 1600s.

Martha was the oldest of eight children. She had three brothers—John, William, and Bartholomew—and four sisters—Anna Maria, Frances, Elizabeth, and Mary. As the first-born daughter, Martha was expected to help with the care of her siblings. Her education was typical for a girl of her class and stressed housekeeping, religion, music, needlework, and dancing; skills that would be useful in her expected role as the wife of a Virginia plantation owner.

As a girl in Virginia, Martha learned to read and write, unlike many women of the time.

She grew into a small, attractive young woman, a little more than five feet tall, with dark hair and eyes. As an adult, she was vivacious, warm, and friendly—the kind of person who drew people to her. One was a gentleman who was twenty years her senior, the heir of one of the wealthiest families in Virginia. Daniel Parke Custis had known Martha since birth, because he was a neighbor and served with her father as a vestryman at their church. Initially, Daniel's father made it clear that he did not want Daniel to marry Martha, because her family did not have the money or the social standing of the Custises. After speaking to Martha, however, John Custis declared that he was as impressed with her intelligence and good sense as his son was with her looks. Martha and Daniel were married on May 15, 1750, just before her nineteenth birthday.

Daniel Parke Custis was Martha's godfather.

The happy couple made their home at Daniel's main plantation, called White House, and grew tobacco for sale in England. Over seven years, Daniel and Martha had four children: Daniel, born in 1751; Frances in 1753; John (Jacky) in 1754; and Martha (Patsy) in 1756. Sadly, the two eldest children died when they were only three and four years old, respectively. While Martha was grieving the loss of her daughter Frances, her husband Daniel suddenly became ill and died in the summer of 1757.

Daniel did not write a will before he died. According to eighteenth-century law in Virginia, the widow had dower rights to the use of one-third of her late husband's estate, including the slaves, for the rest of her life, while the other two-thirds would go to the children when they either reached adulthood or got married. At the death of the widow, her lifetime share would be divided among her late husband's remaining heirs. Daniel left an estate of 17,500 acres of land and almost three hundred slaves.

"I am determined to be cheerful and happy in whatever situation I may find myself. I have also learnt, from experience, that the greater part of our happiness or misery depends upon our dispositions, and not upon our circumstances. We carry the seeds of the one or the other about with us in our minds wherever we go."

Martha Dandridge Custis pulled herself together and began managing Daniel's plantation and business interests. A British colony Virginia, followed English law, which limited married women's abilities to own property. A woman could only own property herself if she was either single or widowed. Married women were legally considered one person with their husband, but the identity of that person was his. This gave Martha the rare opportunity to engage in business on her own.

She wrote to Daniel's agents in England to let them know of his death and that all business issues should come directly to her. Under the economic system in place, the colonies provided raw materials for British merchants and industries, in exchange for manufactured goods from around the world. Martha's money and most goods that she might need came from her husband's agents in England. Martha was exacting and firm in her decisions. She ordered an elaborate tombstone for Daniel and mourning clothes for herself and her remaining children. She ordered supplies to run the business. When those items were not exactly what she had in mind, she wrote to those British agents to complain about the quality of what was sent.

In the spring of 1758, Martha's life took a dramatic turn. Even though Daniel had been dead less than year, it was not uncommon for widows to remarry

Martha had several suitors after Daniel's death.

quickly. The fact that she was young, pretty, rich, and only had two children made her attractive to men who were looking for a wife. At least two men were interested in her. The first was Charles Carter of Cleve, who, like Daniel, was about twenty years older than Martha, wealthy, comfortable in society, and from an important family. He had been widowed twice and was looking for a third wife to fill the role of mother for his large family. From surviving letters, it appears that Charles was confident that Martha would agree to marry him. However, Charles had competition.

According to the story in her grandson George Washington Parke Custis's memoirs, the widow Custis and her two children were visiting the home of their neighbors, the Chamberlaynes, when the master of the house brought home a friend for dinner: Colonel George Washington, the commander of the Virginia Regimen,

George Washington unsuccessfully courted several young women in Virginia and New York and was still a bachelor in 1758.

which protected colonists on a stretch of over three hundred miles of frontier from attacks by the French and their Native American allies during the French and Indian War. Colonel Washington towered over petite Martha. He was about six feet two inches tall, with reddish-brown hair, blue eyes, and an athletic build. Eight months younger than Martha, he was known throughout Britain, France, and the American colonies for his exploits on the frontier.

Washington is said to have told his servant, Thomas Bishop, to rest the horses and they would get back on the road after dinner. Dinner ended in the late afternoon—but the colonel sent word to Bishop to put the horses up because they were staying overnight. Martha's grandson wrote that the reason for this delay was that the colonel was quite taken with the charming widow and her two small children. Within just a couple of months, they made the decision to marry after the new year.

Despite the charming description of the couple's first meeting, it is likely they had met before. As the wife of a prominent Virginia planter and George the hero of the day, Mrs. Custis' and Colonel Washington's paths may have crossed earlier at any number of social engagements in Williamsburg, the capital of Virginia, where they shared friends and acquaintances. Writing to George ten days after their wedding, an army friend noted that all the men in the Virginia Regiment were pleased that their colonel had won the hand of the lady they all knew had "long been the just object of your affections," a clue that the couple had probably known one another for quite some time.

Having just lost one husband, Martha did not want the uncertainty of being married to a soldier. In the months leading up to the wedding, Washington let it

It is possible that Martha met George while she was married to Daniel.

be known that he would be leaving the army. He took part in a final campaign in western Pennsylvania and successfully ran for a seat in the House of Burgesses.

Martha Dandridge Custis and George Washington were married in an Anglican ceremony at the bride's home on January 6, 1759. George Washington brought his new family to live at Mount Vernon, his family plantation since 1674. During the trip, he purchased a peacock, perhaps as a present for Martha, who dearly loved birds (she would later own several parrots). The couple shared a love of dogs, horses, and gardening. They both liked to keep up with current events through reading newspapers. Martha expressed her artistic skills by doing beautiful needlework. She also loved to read, having a special fondness for novels and books on religion. The couple shared a similar faith in God. In keeping with Anglican practice, Martha set aside an hour each morning and evening for Bible reading, prayer, and her private devotions.

The little family settled into a comfortable life at Mount Vernon. George Washington became a gentleman planter, occupied with business affairs and his duties as a church vestryman and local politician. Martha oversaw the domestic staff of both hired and enslaved butlers, housekeepers, maids, cooks, waiters, laundresses, spinners, seamstresses, and gardeners. She looked after the children and supervised their early education.

George and Martha did not have children together, and there was some tension between the Washingtons on the subject of the Custis children. Having lost her first two children, Martha tended to worry and be overprotective, and had a very hard time when she was away from them. At one point, Martha and Patsy went to visit George's brother and his wife. As an experiment, she left Jacky home. The

Martha's youngest granddaughter later recalled that when she really wanted her husband to pay attention to what she was saying, Martha would grab George's lapel and pull his face down to her level.

separation was almost unbearable for her. When a dog barked or she heard a noise, she was sure it was a messenger calling her home because Jacky was ill or had been hurt. George often wanted to take a firmer hand with Jacky, but felt that, as the boy's stepfather, he could not push the issue as he would have with a son of his own. As the children grew older, tutors were hired to teach more difficult subjects, as well as music and dancing. Jacky was eventually sent to a school run by an Anglican minister for more serious studies. A matter of considerable concern to the family was Patsy's fragile health. When she was about twelve years old, Patsy began having seizures, probably a symptom of epilepsy. As a toddler, she had occasionally suffered from "fits & fevours," possible early indicators of these seizures. The Washingtons consulted many doctors and tried an array of medicines and therapies that included an iron ring, soaking in the waters at Warm

Springs, and taking musk capsules, but nothing worked. In one eighty-six-day period, she had seizures on twenty-six days. In 1773, Patsy had a seizure after dinner and died within a few minutes. She was just seventeen years old. George wrote to his brother-in-law that Patsy's death has "reduced my poor wife to the lowest ebb of misery." Eight months later, Martha was still too grief-stricken to attend Jacky's wedding. Even so, Martha and George's strong bond gave her strength to rally and move forward.

These were years of increasing friction between England and the American colonies. The British government needed to raise money to pay for defending the colonies in the French and Indian War. This angered the colonists, because they had no representatives in Parliament. England levied taxes on goods and services, and the colonies responded with import boycotts and complaints about violations

Conflict between England and the American colonies grew in the late 1760s and early 1770s.

of their rights as Englishmen. George Washington became involved in local protest actions and was elected as one of his colony's representatives to the First Continental Congress in 1774. The other Virginia delegates met him at Mount Vernon to travel north to Philadelphia. Edmund Pendleton wrote that he was taken with Martha Washington's spirit, noting that she appeared ready to make any necessary sacrifice. As they rode off, she stood in the doorway and called out, "God be with you gentlemen."

> *"I hope you will stand firm—I know George will."*

Once again, Martha Washington's world was about to change radically. Now in her midforties, she had always been a wife and mother. While she was known in upper-class circles in the colony, she did not have a public role beyond being

Martha spent roughly half of the 103 months of the American Revolution either with her husband in camp, or nearby, in support and to spend more time together.

a gracious hostess to the guests at her home. She had never traveled outside Virginia. In the spring of 1775, the colony of Virginia sent her husband back to the Second Continental Congress. In June, she received two special letters from him. The first broke the news that he had just been made commander of the American military forces gathering outside the British-occupied city of Boston, Massachusetts. George wrote that he did not seek the position and assured her that he would "enjoy more real happiness and felicity in one month with you, at home, than I have the most distant prospect of reaping abroad, if my stay were to be Seven times Seven years." He said that he hoped to be back at Mount Vernon by fall. A week later, he wrote to say that he was getting ready to leave Philadelphia and head for Boston and the army. He told her that neither time nor distance could alter the love he felt for her.

If Martha was shaken by the news that her husband was a soldier once more, she did not share it publicly. The Revolutionary War lasted over eight years, and while her husband commanded the rebel army, she helped George's cousin manage Mount Vernon. She spent almost half of the war in camp with her husband and the army. Those who saw them together commented on the warmth of their relationship. The Marquis de Lafayette described Mrs. Washington as a "modest, respectable woman, who loves her husband madly." Nathanael Greene noted that Martha was "excessive[ly] fond of the General and he of her. They are very happy in each other." Martha Bland, an officer's wife, said that the general's "Worthy Lady seems to be in perfect felicity while she is by the side of her Old Man as she calls him."

Early in the war, smallpox spread rapidly through the country, brought by newly landed British and German soldiers. In-

Many years after the war, one woman recalled Martha at camp, wearing a plain brown homespun dress, and a soldier remembered that, because of a shortage of pins, Martha fastened her clothing with thorns.

oculation was a controversial procedure: a small amount of infectious matter from the sores of a diseased person was placed under the skin of someone who had never had it; then the patient was isolated for about a month, because they were contagious. The result was a milder case of smallpox, a much lower chance of death, and immunity for life from smallpox. A poignant sign of the love Martha felt for her husband was overcoming her fears and, in 1776, undergoing inoculation so she could continue spending time with him and his soldiers in camp. When he learned that she had survived, Jacky wrote to his stepfather that he was happy she "can now attend you to any Part of the Continent with pleasure, unsullied by the Apprehensions of that Disorder . . . this [sic] Consideration has added much to the pleasure I feel on this Occasion, as your Happiness when together will be much greater than when you are apart."

Several years before the war started, Martha had been reluctant to allow her son to be inoculated, for fear that he would die.

In camp, Martha became friends with the wives of the other generals and staff officers.

Besides the comfort she brought to her husband, Martha found a more public role for herself at headquarters. With George preoccupied with military matters, she entertained visiting colonial and international officials and prominent civilians who had come to see the great man or to petition his help. She helped to copy George's correspondence, knitted for the soldiers, and made hospital visits. Martha became a tireless advocate and spokesperson for the plight of the revolutionary soldiers. In 1780, heading home to Mount Vernon following the dreadful second winter at Morristown, New Jersey, Martha stopped to rest for a few days in Philadelphia. Shortly afterwards, Esther DeBerdt Reed, the young wife of a Pennsylvania official, started a campaign challenging women to raise money to help the soldiers. Martha's conversations about her experiences in camp that winter with notable women in Philadelphia spurred them into action.

Martha Washington served as the figurehead of the fund-raising effort: the wife of each governor would collect funds and pass them along to Mrs. Washington at headquarters to distribute to the soldiers. The only surviving letter written by the wife of Virginia governor Thomas Jefferson is a note saying that Mrs. Washington had personally written, asking her to begin organizing the campaign in that state. Concerned that his soldiers would gamble or drink away any gift of currency, Washington convinced the women to purchase shirts, which were desperately needed. In the end, the women purchased fabric and sewed shirts, each embroidered with the name of the woman who made it.

The active military phase of the war ended with the American and French victory over the British at Yorktown, Virginia, in the fall of 1781. The joy of that event was snatched from the Washingtons, when Martha's son, Jacky, who was

State governments and the Continental Congress failed to keep soldiers properly supplied.

The long war finally came to a close at the end of 1783.

acting as a volunteer aide to George, contracted camp fever and died a few weeks later. Just twenty-seven years old, the young man left a widow and four young children. Martha and George were deeply distressed over Jacky's death and his family's grief. It was noted by a friend, "It is certain that they were upon terms of the most affectionate and manly friendship." Over the next two years, George worked hard to keep his army together, as diplomats negotiated a peace treaty. Once that was accomplished, George Washington resigned his commission as commander in chief of the Continental Army and returned home to Mount Vernon on Christmas Eve of 1783. Martha had come back about a month earlier and was waiting to welcome him home.

Over the next few years, George was busy getting Mount Vernon back in shape after his long absence, while he and Martha raised Jacky's younger children:

a little girl named Eleanor Parke Custis (Nelly) and a boy named George Washington Parke Custis (Washy). Their mother and older sisters, Eliza and Patty, frequently came to Mount Vernon to visit. By 1787, George was drawn back into public service as the president of the Constitutional Convention in Philadelphia. After the Constitution was ratified by the newly formed states, the new government was scheduled to launch on March 4, 1789. George Washington was unanimously elected to serve as the first president, but difficulties in getting all the congressmen and senators together delayed the inauguration until several weeks later, on April 30, in the new capital, New York City.

"I little thought, when the war was finished, that any circumstances could possibly have happened, which would call the General into public life again. I had anticipated

*that, from this moment, we should
have been left to grow old, in
solitude and tranquillity, together."*

In the first
years of the
American
government
under the
Constitution,
the capital
was located
in New York
City (1789–
1790) and
Philadelphia
(1790–1800),
before
moving to
the newly
created
city of
Washington,
D.C., in 1800.

Martha and the two grandchildren were
not in New York for the inauguration.
George received official word of his elec-
tion on April 14 and it was going to take
some time for his family to get packed up
and moved. Martha was having a difficult
time accepting that her husband was once
again leaving home to serve the people.
She felt that, at their age and after eight
years away during the Revolution, this
was more than should be asked of them.
Reluctantly she put aside her objections,
dutifully packed up the family, and head-
ed for the new capital.

Once there, Martha again found herself with a public role of her own. Her
husband and his advisers thought that it
was important for the American people to
have access to their president, but that it

needed to be limited to certain times and occasions. They came up with a plan of official entertaining, which allowed people to meet the president but not take his time from important business. On a weekly basis the president hosted a formal reception for gentlemen on Tuesday afternoons; Martha and George had a dinner on Thursday afternoons for members of Congress, local politic ans, diplomats, and their wives; and Martha on Fridays would preside over a levée or reception, an informal function for both ladies and gentlemen, allowing the president to mingle with guests. In a move to prevent accusations of favoritism, Martha was not permitted to pay visits to friends.

"I live a very dull life here and know nothing that passes in the town—I never go to any public place; indeed I think I am more like a state prisoner than anything

else. There are certain bounds set for me which I must not depart from; and as I cannot do as I like, I am obstinate, and stay at home a great deal."

George took Martha and the grandchildren to see a circus elephant on November 16, 1796.

Martha appreciated life in New York and later in Philadelphia, after the capital moved there at the end of 1790. She was happy about the educational opportunities these cities offered to her grandchildren. The family attended concerts, circuses, plays, and museums. There were official visits to factories to promote American manufacturing. Visiting delegations of Native Americans were greeted and entertained in the presidential mansion. Martha's grandson recalled that old soldiers would stop by the official residence and ask to see her; she would have refreshments with them and reminisce about the old days of the war.

George Washington was very much

looking forward to retiring at the end of his first term as president, but he was persuaded by friends and foes alike to stay on for another term; the country was not yet ready for someone else. Nearing the end of his second term, in a long address in the newspapers, George Washington informed the country that he would not accept a third term and would retire on March 4, 1797. Interestingly, given her hesitancy at the start of the presidency, Martha cried as she said goodbye to the people of Philadelphia.

John Adams became the second president of the United States of America. The Washingtons returned to Mount Vernon after the inauguration and spent the next years fixing up their home, welcoming old friends for visits, and enjoying their growing family, as Martha's grandchildren began to marry and produce great-grandchildren. This happy time ended unexpectedly, when George suddenly became

The Washingtons returned to Mount Vernon, hoping for a long, quiet retirement.

ill and died on December 14, 1799. The cause of death was a severe bacterial infection of the epiglottis. His body was placed in the old family vault at Mount Vernon.

Martha was devastated when George died and looked forward to her own death. Visitors to Mount Vernon recalled that she was still the gracious hostess she had always been, but she often noted that she was ready to join her husband. Martha moved from the room she had shared with her husband of forty years to a smaller room on the third floor of the mansion. She never again entered either their bedroom or George's study. Sometime during the next two years, she burned almost all the couple's correspondence to retain the privacy they rarely had in their lives together. Among the projects she undertook during her widowhood was the task of liberating the 123 slaves who belonged to George; they became free on

According to family members, Martha was in such a state of shock that she could not even cry for several weeks after George's death.

January 1, 1801. Unfortunately, she was not able to free the 153 Custis dower slaves, who would become the property of her four grandchildren upon her death. In the spring of 1802, Martha suffered for several weeks from an illness described as "bilious fever." Martha chose a special dress in which to be buried, gave advice to her grandchildren, took communion, and, according to her grandson, "spoke of the happy influences of religion upon the affairs of this world, of the consolations they had afforded her in many and trying afflictions, and of the hopes they held out of a blessed immortality." She died on May 22, 1802, surrounded by her family. Martha was buried beside her beloved husband George.

Through the course of her seventy-one years, Martha's world expanded beyond Virginia and the quiet country life she expected to lead. Her love for George Washington drew her into the wider world,

Alexander Hamilton's widow later said of Martha that "she was always my ideal of a true woman."

bringing her a prominent role in the camps of the Continental Army during the Revolution and later as wife of the first president of the United States. She set a standard of grace and involvement for subsequent First Ladies. Her eulogy proclaimed: "The conjugal, maternal and domestic duties had all been fulfilled in an exemplary manner. She was the worthy partner of the worthiest of men, and those who witnessed their conduct could not determine which excelled in their different characters, both were so well sustained on every occasion. They lived an honor and a pattern to their country, and are taken from us to receive the rewards—promised to the faithful and just."

n. Washington M. Wa
e ton M. Washington
n. Washington M. Wa
e ton M. Washington
n. Washington M. Wa
e ton M. Washington
n. Washington M. Wa
e ton M. Washington
n. Washington M. Wa
e ton M. Washington
n. Washington M. Wa
e ton M. Washington
n. Washington M. Wa